# PRAYER

A 12-MONTH UNDATED PRAYER, SERMON NOTES, AND
REFLECTION JOURNAL FOR ALL AGES AND STAGES

Published by TK Press | Battle Ground, WA
Copyright © 2021 by TK Press.



Permission requests may sent to
TK Press, PO Box 1983, Battle Ground, WA 98604.



To order additional copies of this resource, or request a custom cover
imprint for your organization or group, please visit www.tkpress.com.

Printed in the United States of America.

ISBN-13: 979-8-9851838-0-1

**This book belongs to:**

Name:

_________________________________

Date:

_________________________________

This book is dedicated to ....
GOD, JESUS, and the HOLY SPIRIT,

you,
family,
friends,
neighbors,
co-workers,
teachers,
students,
EVERYONE WHO HAS COME BEFORE,
EVERYONE WHO WILL COME AFTER,
AND EVERYONE IN YOUR SPHERE OF INFLUENCE.

Prayer is a gift
of communication with God
and a blessing
and comfort
to those around us.

May you be open to
receive
what God
has for you
as you
open your
heart
and
mind to
pray,
listen,
and
reflect.

# What's inside?



JOURNAL SECTIONS

- Check-in
- Prayer Log
- Sermon Notes
- Notes & Reflections

"

And pray in the Spirit
on all occasions
with all kinds
of prayers and requests.

With this in mind,
be alert and always
keep on praying
for all the Lord's people.

"

Ephesians 6:18 NIV

# Start here.

### STEP #1 - Own it!

Start by writing your name and the date in the front pages of this book This is an important first step in beginning your prayer journey.

### STEP #2 - Get comfortable.

Take a look at the *What's Inside?* page then look through the book to familiarize yourself with the different sections.

### STEP #3 - Go deeper.

Read through the *You Were Made To...* and *Why Prayer?* pages to learn more about the heart behind this journal and how prayer can help you to better connect with God and those around you.

### STEP #4 - Begin.

Use *Check-In #1* to help you take a snapshot of your current thoughts and feelings.

### STEP #5 - Use regularly.

This undated journal can be started at any time of the year. Each of the 12 sections includes check-in questions; a place to record prayer requests, praises and answers; pages to take sermon notes; and a few pages for notes and reflections.

Lines to write on are included on the *Prayer Request, Sermon Notes, and Notes and Reflection* pages. Lines were left off of the check-in pages to allow freedom in writing size and style, and open space for those who like to add color and drawings in their journals.

## STEP #6 - Reflect.

In addition to the journal sections, there are places to pause and reflect on your prayer journey and relationship with God throughout the year.

These include a *Birthday Reflection*, a *Baptism-Birthday Reflection*, and a *Closing Reflection*.

You'll also find *Scripture References* and *Notes and Reflection* pages toward the back of the book.


## STEP #7 - Rejoice!

*Rejoice in the Lord always. I will say it again: Rejoice!*
*Let your gentleness be evident to all. The Lord is near.*
*Do not be anxious about anything, but in every situation,*
*by prayer and petition, with thanksgiving, present your requests to*
*God. And the peace of God, which transcends all understanding,*
*will guard your hearts and your minds in Christ Jesus.*

*Finally, brothers and sisters, whatever is true, whatever is noble,*
*whatever is right, whatever is pure, whatever is lovely, whatever is*
*admirable—if anything is excellent or praiseworthy—think about such*
*things. Whatever you have learned or received or heard from me, or*
*seen in me—put it into practice. And the God of peace will be with you.*

*- Philippians 4:4-9 NIV*

# You were made to...

## RECEIVE

...peace, love, comfort, kindness, and abundantly more from God as we seek Him, learn more about Him, and walk in His truths.

## GIVE

...to others out of what we've received from God in our roles as spouse, parent, child, friend, neighbor, manager, employee, volunteer...

## Each day, we choose

Life can be hectic, busy, and distracting. Each new day we choose from who, what, and where we will receive guidance, peace, love, kindness, approval, and satisfaction. Are we receiving from friends, family, hobbies, pets, ambitions, achievements, material things, social media, a combination of those, or something else?

When we take time to pray, we open ourselves up to receive God's messages of peace, love, comfort, kindness, redirection, and wisdom.

As we seek Him, our hearts, minds, and lives are open and our ears turned to His voice, so that instead of looking to the world to fulfill our needs, we can listen for and receive "every good and perfect gift" He promises.

Without prayer, we are more likely to look to others, our personal achievements, material possessions, or comfortable habits to receive only a portion of what God has designed for us.

*Every good and perfect gift is from above,*
*coming down from the Father of the heavenly lights,*
*who does not change like shifting shadows.*

- James 1:17 NIV

Is your cup full or empty?

Connecting with God through prayer and receiving what He has
planned for us, allows us to give from a place of
abundance – able to give spiritually, physically, emotionally more than
we could on our own.

If we rely on our personal strength and give out of a sense of duty or
moral responsibility, we are more likely to burn out or struggle in giving
of ourselves, our time, our talents, and efforts.

Are you giving out of a cup that is overflowing with God's blessings or
out of an empty or partially filled cup?

*Because of the Lord's great love we are not*
*consumed, for his compassions never fail. They*
*are new every morning; great is your faithfulness.*

*- Lamentations 3:22-23 NIV*

REFLECTION: From where are you receiving? What do you
receive? How are you giving to others in your life?

Use the space below to reflect and record your thoughts.

# Why prayer?

Have you ever struggled to communicate with someone in your life?
Or given up on a relationship because you lacked the time, energy, and
connection to make it work?  When problems arise, we are naturally
inclined to withdraw, get angry and lash out, or seek further information
and press on in perseverance.

This prayer journal is a tool and guide to encourage you.

As you use it to draw near to God, our hope is that you take in His
peace, kindness, comfort, wisdom and goodness, and when the time is
right, share your experience with others.

Our goal was to create a tool that is helpful at any age or stage –
whether you are new to prayer or a steadfast prayer warrior;
a seeker, new believer, or friend of God.

You'll find answers to some common questions about prayer on the next
page to help you begin.


*And pray in the Spirit on all occasions with all kinds of prayers and
requests. With this in mind, be alert and always keep on praying
for all the Lord's people.*

- Ephesians 6:18

## When should I pray?

Prayer is a personal time of communication between you and God.
There is no right or wrong time to pray. In fact, the Bible calls us to pray
at all times, about all things, and pray without ceasing.

## Do I have to close my eyes?

You will benefit from prayer whether your eyes are open or closed.
If you struggle with attention or focus, try closing your eyes.
Of course, if you pray while walking, driving, or cooking, please
keep your eyes open.

## Do I have to pray out loud?

Some people find praying out loud daunting, while others are in their
element voicing their thoughts and prayers. Praying out loud is not a
requirement, so if you prefer to sit in silence and pray in your head, that
is okay. God hears your prayers – spoken or unspoken. There are times
when I have conversations with God as if He is sitting right next to me
and times when I lay in bed meditating on His word, asking questions,
and listening for His replies.

## I don't know what to say...

There will be times that you will have much to say and times when you
struggle to find the words to pray. Thankfully, God promises that His
Spirit will interpret and intercede for us when we are at a loss for words.


*In the same way, the Spirit helps us in our weakness.*
*We do not know what we ought to pray for, but the Spirit himself*
*intercedes for us through wordless groans.. And he who searches our*
*hearts knows the mind of the Spirit, because the Spirit intercedes for*
*God's people in accordance with the will of God.*

*- Romans 8:26-27*

# Check-in #1

**Date:**

How's it going? This first check-in is to record your thoughts and feelings at the start of this journal and to choose an area of growth to focus on for the next month. Each section begins with a similar check-in so that you can reflect on patterns, praises, and growth in your journey.

The lack of lines to write on in these check-in sections is intentional. While lines are great, open space allows you to own this, writing in a size that is comfortable for you and adding color, drawings, or other embellishments if desired making it unique to you.

## How is my relationship with God right now?

Place a mark on the scale below to show where you're at

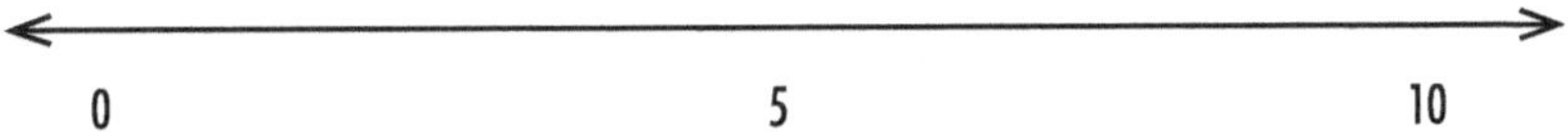



0 = I DON'T YET HAVE A RELATIONSHIP WITH GOD
5 = I KNOW GOD, BUT STRUGGLE TO CONSISTENTLY FOLLOW HIM
10 = I HAVE A GOOD RELATIONSHIP WITH GOD AND SEEK HIM DAILY

## How important is prayer in your life?

Place a mark on the scale below to show where you're at

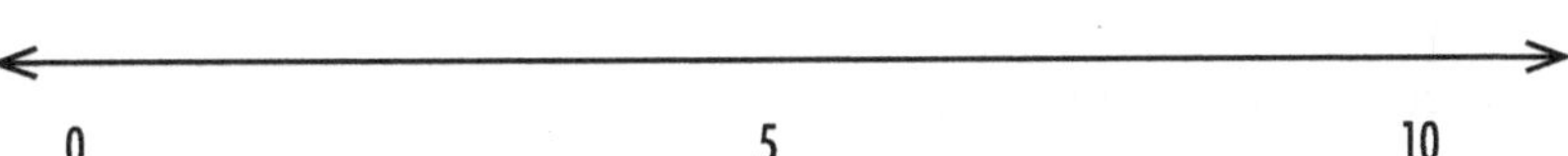



0 = I DON'T REALLY PRAY
5 = I PRAY WHEN I THINK OF IT OR WHEN THERE'S A SPECIFIC NEED
10 = I AM A PRAYER WARRIOR AND PRAY CONTINUOUSLY

What blessings am I grateful for?


What is a struggle or challenge right now?


How is God speaking into my life right now?


My favorite place to pray is:


My favorite time to pray is:

An area of growth I'd like to focus on next month is:

Write a prayer below inviting God to meet you where you are,
to remind you of who you are to Him, and to help you grow
in your relationship with Him.

"

This, then, is how you should pray:
"'Our Father in heaven,
hallowed be your name,
your kingdom come,
your will be done,
on earth as it is in heaven.
Give us today our daily bread.
And forgive us our debts,
as we also have forgiven our debtors.
And lead us not into temptation,
but deliver us from the evil one'

"

Matthew 6:9-13 NIV

# Using the prayer log

Writing down your prayers and prayer requests from others is a great way to keep track of who to pray for, what to pray for, and how God reveals an answer. As you pray and record updates, praises, and answers you will better see how God is working in your life and the lives of those you pray for.

There are Prayer Request pages in each section.
Below is an example of how to use those pages.

**Date:**    February 27, 2021

**Request:**  Jon - job interview with a company closer to home;

Joan - desire to hear God more clearly, learn more about prayer,

and increase gratitude

**Update/Answer:**  PRAISE! Jon was offered the job and asks for continued

prayers as he transitions. UPDATE: Joan and I are meeting for prayer each

week and she is growing in her relationships with God and her family

“

And pray in the Spirit
on all occasions
with all kinds
of prayers and requests.

With this in mind,
be alert and always
keep on praying
for all the Lord's people.

”

Ephesians 6:18 NIV

# Prayer Requests

Date:

Request:

_______________________________________

_______________________________________

_______________________________________

_______________________________________

Update/Answer:

_______________________________________

_______________________________________

_______________________________________

_______________________________________

Date:

Request:

_______________________________________

_______________________________________

_______________________________________

_______________________________________

Update/Answer:

_______________________________________

_______________________________________

_______________________________________

_______________________________________

# Prayer Requests

Date:

Request:

_______________________________

_______________________________

_______________________________

_______________________________

Update/Answer:

_______________________________

_______________________________

_______________________________

Date:

Request:

_______________________________

_______________________________

_______________________________

Update/Answer:

_______________________________

_______________________________

_______________________________

# Prayer Requests

Date:
Request:

_______________________________

_______________________________

_______________________________

_______________________________

Update/Answer:

_______________________________

_______________________________

_______________________________

Date:
Request:

_______________________________

_______________________________

_______________________________

_______________________________

Update/Answer:

_______________________________

_______________________________

_______________________________

# Prayer Requests

Date:

Request:

_______________________________

_______________________________

_______________________________

_______________________________

Update/Answer:

_______________________________

_______________________________

_______________________________

_______________________________

Date:

Request:

_______________________________

_______________________________

_______________________________

_______________________________

Update/Answer:

_______________________________

_______________________________

_______________________________

# Prayer Requests

Date:
Request:

_____________________________________

_____________________________________

_____________________________________

_____________________________________

Update/Answer:

_____________________________________

_____________________________________

_____________________________________

_____________________________________

Date:
Request:

_____________________________________

_____________________________________

_____________________________________

_____________________________________

Update/Answer:

_____________________________________

_____________________________________

_____________________________________

# Prayer Requests

Date:

Request:

Update/Answer:

Date:

Request:

Update/Answer:

# Prayer Requests

**Date:**

**Request:**

_______________________________________________

_______________________________________________

_______________________________________________

_______________________________________________

**Update/Answer:**

_______________________________________________

_______________________________________________

_______________________________________________

_______________________________________________

**Date:**

**Request:**

_______________________________________________

_______________________________________________

_______________________________________________

_______________________________________________

**Update/Answer:**

_______________________________________________

_______________________________________________

_______________________________________________

# Prayer Requests

Date:

Request:

_______________________________

_______________________________

_______________________________

_______________________________

Update/Answer:

_______________________________

_______________________________

_______________________________

_______________________________

Date:

Request:

_______________________________

_______________________________

_______________________________

_______________________________

Update/Answer:

_______________________________

_______________________________

_______________________________

_______________________________

# Prayer Requests

Date:

Request:

__________________________________________

__________________________________________

__________________________________________

__________________________________________

Update/Answer:

__________________________________________

__________________________________________

__________________________________________

__________________________________________

Date:

Request:

__________________________________________

__________________________________________

__________________________________________

Update/Answer:

__________________________________________

__________________________________________

__________________________________________

# Sermon Notes

Date:

Speaker:

# Sermon Notes

Date:

Speaker:

_______________________________________________

_______________________________________________

_______________________________________________

_______________________________________________

_______________________________________________

_______________________________________________

_______________________________________________

_______________________________________________

_______________________________________________

# Sermon Notes

Date:

Speaker:

# Sermon Notes

**Date:**
**Speaker:**

# Notes & Reflections

# Notes & Reflections

“

Answer me when I call to you,
my righteous God.
Give me relief from my distress;
have mercy on me
and hear my prayer.


”

Psalm 4:1 NIV

# Check-in #2

Date:

It's time for a monthly reflection and check-in. Remember that each person's prayer journey is unique and personal. Be honest and take time to reflect on your answers.


## MY PRAYER JOURNEY:

Place a mark on the scale below to show where you're at

$\longleftarrow \qquad\qquad\qquad\qquad\qquad\qquad \longrightarrow$

0          5          10

0 = I DON'T REALLY PRAY
5 = I PRAY WHEN I THINK OF IT OR WHEN THERE'S A SPECIFIC NEED
10 = I AM A PRAYER WARRIOR AND PRAY CONTINUOUSLY


## Today I am... (CIRCLE ONE):

SEEING GROWTH IN MY PRAYER LIFE
STRUGGLING WITH:
OTHER:


## What am I grateful for?

What is challenging right now?




How am I showing kindness to myself and others?




Use the space below to write a prayer or draw a picture
as you think about the month ahead.

# Prayer Requests

Date:

Request:

Update/Answer:

Date:

Request:

Update/Answer:

# Prayer Requests

Date:

Request:

_________________________________________

_________________________________________

_________________________________________

_________________________________________

Update/Answer:

_________________________________________

_________________________________________

_________________________________________

_________________________________________

Date:

Request:

_________________________________________

_________________________________________

_________________________________________

_________________________________________

Update/Answer:

_________________________________________

_________________________________________

_________________________________________

_________________________________________

# Prayer Requests

Date:
Request:

___________________________

___________________________

___________________________

___________________________

Update/Answer:

___________________________

___________________________

___________________________

Date:
Request:

___________________________

___________________________

___________________________

Update/Answer:

___________________________

___________________________

___________________________

# Prayer Requests

Date:

Request:

_______________________________________

_______________________________________

_______________________________________

_______________________________________

Update/Answer:

_______________________________________

_______________________________________

_______________________________________

_______________________________________

Date:

Request:

_______________________________________

_______________________________________

_______________________________________

_______________________________________

Update/Answer:

_______________________________________

_______________________________________

_______________________________________

# Prayer Requests

Date:

Request:

___________________________________

___________________________________

___________________________________

___________________________________

Update/Answer:

___________________________________

___________________________________

___________________________________

___________________________________

Date:

Request:

___________________________________

___________________________________

___________________________________

Update/Answer:

___________________________________

___________________________________

___________________________________

# Prayer Requests

Date:

Request:

_______________________________________

_______________________________________

_______________________________________

_______________________________________

Update/Answer:

_______________________________________

_______________________________________

_______________________________________

_______________________________________

Date:

Request:

_______________________________________

_______________________________________

_______________________________________

_______________________________________

Update/Answer:

_______________________________________

_______________________________________

_______________________________________

_______________________________________

# Prayer Requests

Date:

Request:

____________________________

____________________________

____________________________

____________________________

Update/Answer:

____________________________

____________________________

____________________________

____________________________

Date:

Request:

____________________________

____________________________

____________________________

____________________________

Update/Answer:

____________________________

____________________________

____________________________

# Prayer Requests

Date:

Request:

___

___

___

___

Update/Answer:

___

___

___

___

Date:

Request:

___

___

___

___

Update/Answer:

___

___

___

___

# Sermon Notes

Date:

Speaker:

# Sermon Notes

Date:

Speaker:

# Sermon Notes

Date:

Speaker:

# Sermon Notes

Date:

Speaker:

# Sermon Notes

Date:

Speaker:

# Notes & Reflections

# Notes & Reflections

**"**

If my people,
who are called by my name,
will humble themselves
and pray and seek my face
and turn from their wicked ways,
then I will hear from heaven,
and I will forgive their sin
and will heal their land.

**"**

2 Chronicles 7:14 NIV

# Check-in #3

Date:

It's time for a monthly reflection and check-in. Remember that each person's prayer journey is unique and personal. Be honest and take time to reflect on your answers.

## MY PRAYER JOURNEY:

Place a mark on the scale below to show where you're at

$\longleftrightarrow$

0               5               10

0 = I DON'T REALLY PRAY
5 = I PRAY WHEN I THINK OF IT OR WHEN THERE'S A SPECIFIC NEED
10 = I AM A PRAYER WARRIOR AND PRAY CONTINUOUSLY

## Today I am... (CIRCLE ONE):

SEEING GROWTH IN MY PRAYER LIFE
STRUGGLING WITH:
OTHER:

## What am I grateful for?

What is challenging right now?

How am I showing kindness to myself and others?

Use the space below to write a prayer or draw a picture
as you think about the month ahead.

# Prayer Requests

Date:

Request:

_______________________________________

_______________________________________

_______________________________________

_______________________________________

Update/Answer:

_______________________________________

_______________________________________

_______________________________________

_______________________________________

Date:

Request:

_______________________________________

_______________________________________

_______________________________________

_______________________________________

Update/Answer:

_______________________________________

_______________________________________

_______________________________________

# Prayer Requests

Date:
Request:

________________________

________________________

________________________

________________________

Update/Answer:

________________________

________________________

________________________

________________________

Date:
Request:

________________________

________________________

________________________

________________________

Update/Answer:

________________________

________________________

________________________

________________________

# Prayer Requests

Date:

Request:

___

Update/Answer:

___

Date:

Request:

___

Update/Answer:

___

# Prayer Requests

Date:

Request:

_______________________________

_______________________________

_______________________________

Update/Answer:

_______________________________

_______________________________

_______________________________

Date:

Request:

_______________________________

_______________________________

_______________________________

Update/Answer:

_______________________________

_______________________________

_______________________________

# Prayer Requests

Date:

Request:

Update/Answer:

Date:

Request:

Update/Answer:

# Prayer Requests

Date:

Request:

_______________________________

_______________________________

_______________________________

_______________________________

Update/Answer:

_______________________________

_______________________________

_______________________________

Date:

Request:

_______________________________

_______________________________

_______________________________

_______________________________

Update/Answer:

_______________________________

_______________________________

_______________________________

# Prayer Requests

Date:

Request:

_______________________________

_______________________________

_______________________________

_______________________________

Update/Answer:

_______________________________

_______________________________

_______________________________

_______________________________

Date:

Request:

_______________________________

_______________________________

_______________________________

_______________________________

Update/Answer:

_______________________________

_______________________________

_______________________________

_______________________________

# Prayer Requests

Date:
Request:

_______________________________________

_______________________________________

_______________________________________

_______________________________________

Update/Answer:

_______________________________________

_______________________________________

_______________________________________

_______________________________________

Date:
Request:

_______________________________________

_______________________________________

_______________________________________

_______________________________________

Update/Answer:

_______________________________________

_______________________________________

_______________________________________

_______________________________________

# Sermon Notes

Date:

Speaker:

# Sermon Notes

Date:

Speaker:

# Sermon Notes

Date:

Speaker:

# Sermon Notes

Date:
Speaker:

# Sermon Notes

Date:

Speaker:

# Notes & Reflections

# Notes & Reflections

"

Do not be anxious about anything,
but in every situation,
by prayer and petition,
with thanksgiving,
present your requests to God.

"

Philippians 4:6 NIV

# Check-in #4

Date:

It's time for a monthly reflection and check-in. Remember that each person's prayer journey is unique and personal. Be honest and take time to reflect on your answers.


## MY PRAYER JOURNEY:

Place a mark on the scale below to show where you're at

← ─────────────────────────────────────────────── →

0                              5                              10

    0 = I DON'T REALLY PRAY
    5 = I PRAY WHEN I THINK OF IT OR WHEN THERE'S A SPECIFIC NEED
    10 = I AM A PRAYER WARRIOR AND PRAY CONTINUOUSLY


## Today I am... (CIRCLE ONE):

SEEING GROWTH IN MY PRAYER LIFE
STRUGGLING WITH:
OTHER:


## What am I grateful for?

What is challenging right now?

How am I showing kindness to myself and others?

Use the space below to write a prayer or draw a picture
as you think about the month ahead.

# Prayer Requests

Date:

Request:

---

---

---

---

Update/Answer:

---

---

---

---

Date:

Request:

---

---

---

---

Update/Answer:

---

---

---

---

# Prayer Requests

Date:

Request:

_______________________________

_______________________________

_______________________________

_______________________________

Update/Answer:

_______________________________

_______________________________

_______________________________

_______________________________

Date:

Request:

_______________________________

_______________________________

_______________________________

_______________________________

Update/Answer:

_______________________________

_______________________________

_______________________________

# Prayer Requests

Date:

Request:

_______________________________

_______________________________

_______________________________

_______________________________

Update/Answer:

_______________________________

_______________________________

_______________________________

_______________________________

Date:

Request:

_______________________________

_______________________________

_______________________________

_______________________________

Update/Answer:

_______________________________

_______________________________

_______________________________

_______________________________

# Prayer Requests

Date:
Request:

_______________________________

_______________________________

_______________________________

_______________________________

Update/Answer:

_______________________________

_______________________________

_______________________________

Date:
Request:

_______________________________

_______________________________

_______________________________

_______________________________

Update/Answer:

_______________________________

_______________________________

_______________________________

# Prayer Requests

Date:

Request:

_______________________________________

_______________________________________

_______________________________________

_______________________________________

Update/Answer:

_______________________________________

_______________________________________

_______________________________________

_______________________________________

Date:

Request:

_______________________________________

_______________________________________

_______________________________________

_______________________________________

Update/Answer:

_______________________________________

_______________________________________

_______________________________________

_______________________________________

# Prayer Requests

Date:

Request:

_______________________________________

_______________________________________

_______________________________________

_______________________________________

Update/Answer:

_______________________________________

_______________________________________

_______________________________________

_______________________________________

Date:

Request:

_______________________________________

_______________________________________

_______________________________________

_______________________________________

Update/Answer:

_______________________________________

_______________________________________

_______________________________________

_______________________________________

# Prayer Requests

Date:

Request:

_______________________________________________

_______________________________________________

_______________________________________________

_______________________________________________

Update/Answer:

_______________________________________________

_______________________________________________

_______________________________________________

_______________________________________________

Date:

Request:

_______________________________________________

_______________________________________________

_______________________________________________

_______________________________________________

Update/Answer:

_______________________________________________

_______________________________________________

_______________________________________________

_______________________________________________

# Prayer Requests

Date:

Request:

________________________________

________________________________

________________________________

________________________________

Update/Answer:

________________________________

________________________________

________________________________

________________________________

Date:

Request:

________________________________

________________________________

________________________________

________________________________

Update/Answer:

________________________________

________________________________

________________________________

________________________________

# Sermon Notes

Date:
Speaker:

# Sermon Notes

Date:
Speaker:

# Sermon Notes

Date:

Speaker:

# Sermon Notes

Date:
Speaker:

# Sermon Notes

Date:

Speaker:

# Notes & Reflections

# Notes & Reflections

"

In the same way,
the Spirit helps us
in our weakness.
We do not know
what we ought to pray for,
but the Spirit himself
intercedes for us
through wordless groans.

"

Romans 8:26 NIV

# Check-in #5

Date:

It's time for a monthly reflection and check-in. Remember that each person's prayer journey is unique and personal. Be honest and take time to reflect on your answers.


## MY PRAYER JOURNEY:

Place a mark on the scale below to show where you're at

$$\longleftarrow \longrightarrow$$

0                                          5                                          10

0 = I DON'T REALLY PRAY
5 = I PRAY WHEN I THINK OF IT OR WHEN THERE'S A SPECIFIC NEED
10 = I AM A PRAYER WARRIOR AND PRAY CONTINUOUSLY


## Today I am... (CIRCLE ONE):

SEEING GROWTH IN MY PRAYER LIFE
STRUGGLING WITH:
OTHER:


## What am I grateful for?

What is challenging right now?

How am I showing kindness to myself and others?

Use the space below to write a prayer or draw a picture
as you think about the month ahead.

# Prayer Requests

Date:

Request:

_______________________________

_______________________________

_______________________________

_______________________________

Update/Answer:

_______________________________

_______________________________

_______________________________

_______________________________

Date:

Request:

_______________________________

_______________________________

_______________________________

_______________________________

Update/Answer:

_______________________________

_______________________________

_______________________________

_______________________________

# Prayer Requests

Date:
Request:

_______________________________

_______________________________

_______________________________

_______________________________

Update/Answer:

_______________________________

_______________________________

_______________________________

Date:
Request:

_______________________________

_______________________________

_______________________________

Update/Answer:

_______________________________

_______________________________

_______________________________

# Prayer Requests

Date:

Request:

_______________________________

_______________________________

_______________________________

Update/Answer:

_______________________________

_______________________________

_______________________________

Date:

Request:

_______________________________

_______________________________

_______________________________

Update/Answer:

_______________________________

_______________________________

_______________________________

# Prayer Requests

Date:
Request:

_______________________________

_______________________________

_______________________________

_______________________________

Update/Answer:

_______________________________

_______________________________

_______________________________

_______________________________

Date:
Request:

_______________________________

_______________________________

_______________________________

_______________________________

Update/Answer:

_______________________________

_______________________________

_______________________________

# Prayer Requests

Date:

Request:

_______________________________________

_______________________________________

_______________________________________

_______________________________________

Update/Answer:

_______________________________________

_______________________________________

_______________________________________

_______________________________________

Date:

Request:

_______________________________________

_______________________________________

_______________________________________

Update/Answer:

_______________________________________

_______________________________________

_______________________________________

# Prayer Requests

Date:
Request:

________________________

________________________

________________________

________________________

Update/Answer:

________________________

________________________

________________________

________________________

Date:
Request:

________________________

________________________

________________________

________________________

Update/Answer:

________________________

________________________

________________________

________________________

# Prayer Requests

Date:

Request:

_______________________________________

_______________________________________

_______________________________________

_______________________________________

Update/Answer:

_______________________________________

_______________________________________

_______________________________________

_______________________________________

Date:

Request:

_______________________________________

_______________________________________

_______________________________________

_______________________________________

Update/Answer:

_______________________________________

_______________________________________

_______________________________________

# Prayer Requests

Date:

Request:

___________________________________

___________________________________

___________________________________

___________________________________

Update/Answer:

___________________________________

___________________________________

___________________________________

___________________________________

Date:

Request:

___________________________________

___________________________________

___________________________________

___________________________________

Update/Answer:

___________________________________

___________________________________

___________________________________

___________________________________

# Sermon Notes

Date:

Speaker:

# Sermon Notes

Date:
Speaker:

# Sermon Notes

**Date:**

**Speaker:**

# Sermon Notes

Date:

Speaker:

# Sermon Notes

Date:

Speaker:

# Notes & Reflections

# Notes & Reflections

"

Then Jesus told
his disciples a parable
to show them
that they should always pray
and not give up.

"

Luke 18:1 NIV

# Check-in #6

Date:

It's time for a monthly reflection and check-in. Remember that each person's prayer journey is unique and personal. Be honest and take time to reflect on your answers.

## MY PRAYER JOURNEY:

Place a mark on the scale below to show where you're at

$\longleftarrow \qquad\qquad\qquad\qquad\qquad\qquad \longrightarrow$

0            5            10

0 = I DON'T REALLY PRAY
5 = I PRAY WHEN I THINK OF IT OR WHEN THERE'S A SPECIFIC NEED
10 = I AM A PRAYER WARRIOR AND PRAY CONTINUOUSLY

## Today I am... (CIRCLE ONE):

SEEING GROWTH IN MY PRAYER LIFE
STRUGGLING WITH:
OTHER:

## What am I grateful for?

What is challenging right now?




How am I showing kindness to myself and others?




Use the space below to write a prayer or draw a picture
as you think about the month ahead.

# Prayer Requests

Date:

Request:

Update/Answer:

Date:

Request:

Update/Answer:

# Prayer Requests

Date:

Request:

Update/Answer:

Date:

Request:

Update/Answer:

# Prayer Requests

Date:

Request:

________________________________________

________________________________________

________________________________________

________________________________________

Update/Answer:

________________________________________

________________________________________

________________________________________

________________________________________

Date:

Request:

________________________________________

________________________________________

________________________________________

________________________________________

Update/Answer:

________________________________________

________________________________________

________________________________________

# Prayer Requests

Date:
Request:

Update/Answer:

Date:
Request:

Update/Answer:

# Prayer Requests

Date:

Request:

_______________________________________

_______________________________________

_______________________________________

_______________________________________

Update/Answer:

_______________________________________

_______________________________________

_______________________________________

_______________________________________

Date:

Request:

_______________________________________

_______________________________________

_______________________________________

_______________________________________

Update/Answer:

_______________________________________

_______________________________________

_______________________________________

_______________________________________

# Prayer Requests

Date:

Request:

_______________________________________

_______________________________________

_______________________________________

_______________________________________

Update/Answer:

_______________________________________

_______________________________________

_______________________________________

_______________________________________

Date:

Request:

_______________________________________

_______________________________________

_______________________________________

_______________________________________

Update/Answer:

_______________________________________

_______________________________________

_______________________________________

_______________________________________

# Prayer Requests

**Date:**

**Request:**

_______________________________________________

_______________________________________________

_______________________________________________

_______________________________________________

**Update/Answer:**

_______________________________________________

_______________________________________________

_______________________________________________

_______________________________________________

**Date:**

**Request:**

_______________________________________________

_______________________________________________

_______________________________________________

_______________________________________________

**Update/Answer:**

_______________________________________________

_______________________________________________

_______________________________________________

# Prayer Requests

Date:

Request:

_______________________________________

_______________________________________

_______________________________________

_______________________________________

Update/Answer:

_______________________________________

_______________________________________

_______________________________________

_______________________________________

Date:

Request:

_______________________________________

_______________________________________

_______________________________________

_______________________________________

Update/Answer:

_______________________________________

_______________________________________

_______________________________________

_______________________________________

# Sermon Notes

Date:

Speaker:

# Sermon Notes

Date:
Speaker:

# Sermon Notes

Date:

Speaker:

# Sermon Notes

Date:

Speaker:

# Sermon Notes

Date:

Speaker:

# Notes & Reflections

# Notes & Reflections

66

Devote yourselves
to prayer,
being watchful
and thankful.

99

Colossians 4:2 NIV

# Check-in #7

Date:

It's time for a monthly reflection and check-in. Remember that each person's prayer journey is unique and personal. Be honest and take time to reflect on your answers.


## MY PRAYER JOURNEY:

Place a mark on the scale below to show where you're at

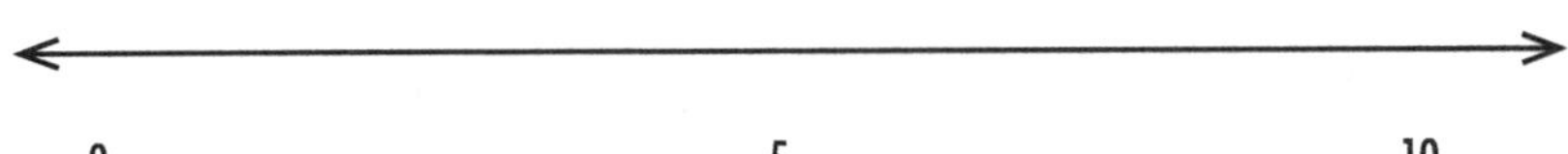

0            5            10

0 = I DON'T REALLY PRAY
5 = I PRAY WHEN I THINK OF IT OR WHEN THERE'S A SPECIFIC NEED
10 = I AM A PRAYER WARRIOR AND PRAY CONTINUOUSLY


## Today I am... (CIRCLE ONE):

SEEING GROWTH IN MY PRAYER LIFE
STRUGGLING WITH:
OTHER:


## What am I grateful for?

What is challenging right now?


How am I showing kindness to myself and others?



Use the space below to write a prayer or draw a picture
as you think about the month ahead.

# Prayer Requests

Date:

Request:

______________________________________

______________________________________

______________________________________

______________________________________

Update/Answer:

______________________________________

______________________________________

______________________________________

______________________________________

Date:

Request:

______________________________________

______________________________________

______________________________________

______________________________________

Update/Answer:

______________________________________

______________________________________

______________________________________

# Prayer Requests

Date:

Request:

___________________________________

___________________________________

___________________________________

___________________________________

Update/Answer:

___________________________________

___________________________________

___________________________________

___________________________________

Date:

Request:

___________________________________

___________________________________

___________________________________

___________________________________

Update/Answer:

___________________________________

___________________________________

___________________________________

___________________________________

# Prayer Requests

Date:

Request:

_______________________________

_______________________________

_______________________________

_______________________________

Update/Answer:

_______________________________

_______________________________

_______________________________

Date:

Request:

_______________________________

_______________________________

_______________________________

Update/Answer:

_______________________________

_______________________________

_______________________________

# Prayer Requests

Date:

Request:

_______________________________________________

_______________________________________________

_______________________________________________

_______________________________________________

Update/Answer:

_______________________________________________

_______________________________________________

_______________________________________________

_______________________________________________

Date:

Request:

_______________________________________________

_______________________________________________

_______________________________________________

_______________________________________________

Update/Answer:

_______________________________________________

_______________________________________________

_______________________________________________

_______________________________________________

# Prayer Requests

Date:

Request:

_______________________________________________

_______________________________________________

_______________________________________________

_______________________________________________

Update/Answer:

_______________________________________________

_______________________________________________

_______________________________________________

Date:

Request:

_______________________________________________

_______________________________________________

_______________________________________________

Update/Answer:

_______________________________________________

_______________________________________________

_______________________________________________

# Prayer Requests

Date:

Request:

_______________________________________

_______________________________________

_______________________________________

_______________________________________

Update/Answer:

_______________________________________

_______________________________________

_______________________________________

_______________________________________

Date:

Request:

_______________________________________

_______________________________________

_______________________________________

_______________________________________

Update/Answer:

_______________________________________

_______________________________________

_______________________________________

_______________________________________

# Prayer Requests

**Date:**

**Request:**

_________________________________________________________

_________________________________________________________

_________________________________________________________

**Update/Answer:**

_________________________________________________________

_________________________________________________________

_________________________________________________________

**Date:**

**Request:**

_________________________________________________________

_________________________________________________________

_________________________________________________________

**Update/Answer:**

_________________________________________________________

_________________________________________________________

_________________________________________________________

# Prayer Requests

Date:

Request:

_______________________________________________

_______________________________________________

_______________________________________________

_______________________________________________

Update/Answer:

_______________________________________________

_______________________________________________

_______________________________________________

_______________________________________________

Date:

Request:

_______________________________________________

_______________________________________________

_______________________________________________

_______________________________________________

Update/Answer:

_______________________________________________

_______________________________________________

_______________________________________________

_______________________________________________

# Sermon Notes

Date:

Speaker:

# Sermon Notes

Date:
Speaker:

# Sermon Notes

**Date:**

**Speaker:**

# Sermon Notes

Date:

Speaker:

# Sermon Notes

**Date:**

**Speaker:**

# Notes & Reflections

# Notes & Reflections

They devoted themselves
to the apostles' teaching
and to fellowship,
to the breaking of bread
and to prayer.

Acts 2:42 NIV

# Check-in #8

Date:

It's time for a monthly reflection and check-in. Remember that each person's prayer journey is unique and personal. Be honest and take time to reflect on your answers.


## MY PRAYER JOURNEY:

Place a mark on the scale below to show where you're at

$$\longleftarrow \hspace{8cm} \longrightarrow$$

0                              5                              10

    0 = I DON'T REALLY PRAY
    5 = I PRAY WHEN I THINK OF IT OR WHEN THERE'S A SPECIFIC NEED
    10 = I AM A PRAYER WARRIOR AND PRAY CONTINUOUSLY


## Today I am... (CIRCLE ONE):

SEEING GROWTH IN MY PRAYER LIFE
STRUGGLING WITH:
OTHER:


## What am I grateful for?

What is challenging right now?




How am I showing kindness to myself and others?




Use the space below to write a prayer or draw a picture
as you think about the month ahead.

# Prayer Requests

Date:

Request:

_______________________________________

_______________________________________

_______________________________________

_______________________________________

Update/Answer:

_______________________________________

_______________________________________

_______________________________________

_______________________________________

Date:

Request:

_______________________________________

_______________________________________

_______________________________________

_______________________________________

Update/Answer:

_______________________________________

_______________________________________

_______________________________________

_______________________________________

# Prayer Requests

Date:

Request:

_______________________________

_______________________________

_______________________________

_______________________________

Update/Answer:

_______________________________

_______________________________

_______________________________

_______________________________

Date:

Request:

_______________________________

_______________________________

_______________________________

_______________________________

Update/Answer:

_______________________________

_______________________________

_______________________________

_______________________________

# Prayer Requests

Date:

Request:

_______________________________________

_______________________________________

_______________________________________

_______________________________________

Update/Answer:

_______________________________________

_______________________________________

_______________________________________

_______________________________________

Date:

Request:

_______________________________________

_______________________________________

_______________________________________

Update/Answer:

_______________________________________

_______________________________________

_______________________________________

# Prayer Requests

**Date:**

**Request:**

_______________________________

_______________________________

_______________________________

_______________________________

**Update/Answer:**

_______________________________

_______________________________

_______________________________

_______________________________

**Date:**

**Request:**

_______________________________

_______________________________

_______________________________

_______________________________

**Update/Answer:**

_______________________________

_______________________________

_______________________________

_______________________________

# Prayer Requests

Date:

Request:

_______________________________

_______________________________

_______________________________

_______________________________

Update/Answer:

_______________________________

_______________________________

_______________________________

_______________________________

Date:

Request:

_______________________________

_______________________________

_______________________________

_______________________________

Update/Answer:

_______________________________

_______________________________

_______________________________

_______________________________

# Prayer Requests

Date:

Request:

_______________________________

_______________________________

_______________________________

_______________________________

Update/Answer:

_______________________________

_______________________________

_______________________________

_______________________________

Date:

Request:

_______________________________

_______________________________

_______________________________

Update/Answer:

_______________________________

_______________________________

_______________________________

# Prayer Requests

Date:

Request:

Update/Answer:

Date:

Request:

Update/Answer:

# Prayer Requests

Date:

Request:

_______________________________

_______________________________

_______________________________

_______________________________

Update/Answer:

_______________________________

_______________________________

_______________________________

_______________________________

Date:

Request:

_______________________________

_______________________________

_______________________________

_______________________________

Update/Answer:

_______________________________

_______________________________

_______________________________

_______________________________

# Sermon Notes

Date:

Speaker:

# Sermon Notes

Date:

Speaker:

# Sermon Notes

**Date:**

**Speaker:**

# Sermon Notes

Date:
Speaker:

# Sermon Notes

Date:

Speaker:

# Notes & Reflections

# Notes & Reflections

"

Ask
and it will be given to you;
seek and you will find;
knock and the door
will be opened to you.
For everyone who asks receives;
the one who seeks finds;
and to the one who knocks,
the door will be opened.

"

Matthew 7:7-8 NIV

# Check-in #9

Date:

It's time for a monthly reflection and check-in. Remember that each person's prayer journey is unique and personal. Be honest and take time to reflect on your answers.


## MY PRAYER JOURNEY:

Place a mark on the scale below to show where you're at

⟵——————————————————————————⟶

0                     5                     10

0 = I DON'T REALLY PRAY
5 = I PRAY WHEN I THINK OF IT OR WHEN THERE'S A SPECIFIC NEED
10 = I AM A PRAYER WARRIOR AND PRAY CONTINUOUSLY


## Today I am... (CIRCLE ONE):

SEEING GROWTH IN MY PRAYER LIFE
STRUGGLING WITH:
OTHER:


## What am I grateful for?

What is challenging right now?

How am I showing kindness to myself and others?

Use the space below to write a prayer or draw a picture
as you think about the month ahead.

# Prayer Requests

Date:
Request:

________________

________________

________________

________________

Update/Answer:

________________

________________

________________

________________

Date:
Request:

________________

________________

________________

________________

Update/Answer:

________________

________________

________________

________________

# Prayer Requests

Date:
Request:

_______________________________________

_______________________________________

_______________________________________

_______________________________________

Update/Answer:

_______________________________________

_______________________________________

_______________________________________

Date:
Request:

_______________________________________

_______________________________________

_______________________________________

Update/Answer:

_______________________________________

_______________________________________

_______________________________________

# Prayer Requests

Date:

Request:

_______________________________________

_______________________________________

_______________________________________

_______________________________________

Update/Answer:

_______________________________________

_______________________________________

_______________________________________

Date:

Request:

_______________________________________

_______________________________________

_______________________________________

_______________________________________

Update/Answer:

_______________________________________

_______________________________________

_______________________________________

# Prayer Requests

Date:

Request:

_________________________________________

_________________________________________

_________________________________________

_________________________________________

Update/Answer:

_________________________________________

_________________________________________

_________________________________________

Date:

Request:

_________________________________________

_________________________________________

_________________________________________

Update/Answer:

_________________________________________

_________________________________________

_________________________________________

# Prayer Requests

Date:
Request:

_________________________________

_________________________________

_________________________________

_________________________________

Update/Answer:

_________________________________

_________________________________

_________________________________

_________________________________

Date:
Request:

_________________________________

_________________________________

_________________________________

_________________________________

Update/Answer:

_________________________________

_________________________________

_________________________________

_________________________________

# Prayer Requests

Date:

Request:

_______________________________________

_______________________________________

_______________________________________

_______________________________________

Update/Answer:

_______________________________________

_______________________________________

_______________________________________

_______________________________________

Date:

Request:

_______________________________________

_______________________________________

_______________________________________

_______________________________________

Update/Answer:

_______________________________________

_______________________________________

_______________________________________

_______________________________________

# Prayer Requests

Date:

Request:

_______________________________________________

_______________________________________________

_______________________________________________

_______________________________________________

Update/Answer:

_______________________________________________

_______________________________________________

_______________________________________________

Date:

Request:

_______________________________________________

_______________________________________________

_______________________________________________

_______________________________________________

Update/Answer:

_______________________________________________

_______________________________________________

_______________________________________________

# Prayer Requests

**Date:**

**Request:**

_______________________________________

_______________________________________

_______________________________________

**Update/Answer:**

_______________________________________

_______________________________________

_______________________________________

**Date:**

**Request:**

_______________________________________

_______________________________________

_______________________________________

**Update/Answer:**

_______________________________________

_______________________________________

_______________________________________

# Sermon Notes

Date:

Speaker:

# Sermon Notes

Date:

Speaker:

# Sermon Notes

Date:

Speaker:

_______________________________________________

_______________________________________________

_______________________________________________

_______________________________________________

_______________________________________________

_______________________________________________

_______________________________________________

_______________________________________________

_______________________________________________

# Sermon Notes

Date:

Speaker:

________________________________________

________________________________________

________________________________________

________________________________________

________________________________________

________________________________________

________________________________________

________________________________________

________________________________________

________________________________________

# Sermon Notes

**Date:**

**Speaker:**

# Notes & Reflections

# Notes & Reflections

But I tell you,
love your enemies
and pray for those
who persecute you,
that you may be children
of your Father in heaven.

Matthew 5:44-45 NIV

# Check-in #10

Date:

It's time for a monthly reflection and check-in. Remember that each person's prayer journey is unique and personal. Be honest and take time to reflect on your answers.


## MY PRAYER JOURNEY:

Place a mark on the scale below to show where you're at

← ———————————————————————————————— →

0                                  5                                  10

    0 = I DON'T REALLY PRAY
    5 = I PRAY WHEN I THINK OF IT OR WHEN THERE'S A SPECIFIC NEED
    10 = I AM A PRAYER WARRIOR AND PRAY CONTINUOUSLY


## Today I am... (CIRCLE ONE):

SEEING GROWTH IN MY PRAYER LIFE
STRUGGLING WITH:
OTHER:


## What am I grateful for?

What is challenging right now?

How am I showing kindness to myself and others?

Use the space below to write a prayer or draw a picture
as you think about the month ahead.

# Prayer Requests

Date:

Request:

Update/Answer:

Date:

Request:

Update/Answer:

# Prayer Requests

Date:
Request:

Update/Answer:

Date:
Request:

Update/Answer:

# Prayer Requests

**Date:**

**Request:**

_______________________________

_______________________________

_______________________________

_______________________________

**Update/Answer:**

_______________________________

_______________________________

_______________________________

**Date:**

**Request:**

_______________________________

_______________________________

_______________________________

**Update/Answer:**

_______________________________

_______________________________

_______________________________

# Prayer Requests

Date:

Request:

_______________________________________

_______________________________________

_______________________________________

_______________________________________

Update/Answer:

_______________________________________

_______________________________________

_______________________________________

_______________________________________

Date:

Request:

_______________________________________

_______________________________________

_______________________________________

_______________________________________

Update/Answer:

_______________________________________

_______________________________________

_______________________________________

_______________________________________

# Prayer Requests

Date:

Request:

_______________________________

_______________________________

_______________________________

_______________________________

Update/Answer:

_______________________________

_______________________________

_______________________________

Date:

Request:

_______________________________

_______________________________

_______________________________

Update/Answer:

_______________________________

_______________________________

_______________________________

# Prayer Requests

**Date:**

**Request:**

_______________________________________________

_______________________________________________

_______________________________________________

_______________________________________________

**Update/Answer:**

_______________________________________________

_______________________________________________

_______________________________________________

_______________________________________________

**Date:**

**Request:**

_______________________________________________

_______________________________________________

_______________________________________________

_______________________________________________

**Update/Answer:**

_______________________________________________

_______________________________________________

_______________________________________________

_______________________________________________

# Prayer Requests

Date:

Request:

___________________________________

___________________________________

___________________________________

___________________________________

Update/Answer:

___________________________________

___________________________________

___________________________________

___________________________________

Date:

Request:

___________________________________

___________________________________

___________________________________

___________________________________

Update/Answer:

___________________________________

___________________________________

___________________________________

# Prayer Requests

Date:
Request:

_______________________________________

_______________________________________

_______________________________________

_______________________________________

Update/Answer:

_______________________________________

_______________________________________

_______________________________________

_______________________________________

Date:
Request:

_______________________________________

_______________________________________

_______________________________________

_______________________________________

Update/Answer:

_______________________________________

_______________________________________

_______________________________________

_______________________________________

# Sermon Notes

Date:

Speaker:

_______________________________________________

_______________________________________________

_______________________________________________

_______________________________________________

_______________________________________________

_______________________________________________

_______________________________________________

_______________________________________________

_______________________________________________

# Sermon Notes

Date:

Speaker:

# Sermon Notes

Date:

Speaker:

# Sermon Notes

Date:

Speaker:

# Sermon Notes

Date:

Speaker:

# Notes & Reflections

# Notes & Reflections

You, God, are my God,
earnestly I seek you;
I thirst for you,
my whole being longs for you,
in a dry and parched land
where there is no water.

I have seen you in the sanctuary
and beheld your power and your glory.
Because your love is better than life,
my lips will glorify you.
I will praise you as long as I live,
and in your name I will lift up my hands.
I will be fully satisfied as with the richest of foods;
with singing lips my mouth will praise you.

On my bed I remember you;
I think of you through the watches of the night.
Because you are my help,
I sing in the shadow of your wings.
I cling to you; your right hand upholds me.

**Psalm 63:1-8 NIV**

# Check-in #11

Date:

It's time for a monthly reflection and check-in. Remember that each person's prayer journey is unique and personal. Be honest and take time to reflect on your answers.

## MY PRAYER JOURNEY:

Place a mark on the scale below to show where you're at

| 0 | 5 | 10 |

0 = I DON'T REALLY PRAY
5 = I PRAY WHEN I THINK OF IT OR WHEN THERE'S A SPECIFIC NEED
10 = I AM A PRAYER WARRIOR AND PRAY CONTINUOUSLY

## Today I am... (CIRCLE ONE):

SEEING GROWTH IN MY PRAYER LIFE
STRUGGLING WITH:
OTHER:

## What am I grateful for?

What is challenging right now?




How am I showing kindness to myself and others?




Use the space below to write a prayer or draw a picture
as you think about the month ahead.

# Prayer Requests

Date:

Request:

_______________________________________

_______________________________________

_______________________________________

_______________________________________

Update/Answer:

_______________________________________

_______________________________________

_______________________________________

_______________________________________

Date:

Request:

_______________________________________

_______________________________________

_______________________________________

_______________________________________

Update/Answer:

_______________________________________

_______________________________________

_______________________________________

_______________________________________

# Prayer Requests

**Date:**

**Request:**

__________________________________________________________

__________________________________________________________

__________________________________________________________

**Update/Answer:**

__________________________________________________________

__________________________________________________________

__________________________________________________________

**Date:**

**Request:**

__________________________________________________________

__________________________________________________________

__________________________________________________________

**Update/Answer:**

__________________________________________________________

__________________________________________________________

__________________________________________________________

# Prayer Requests

Date:

Request:

_______________________________

_______________________________

_______________________________

_______________________________

Update/Answer:

_______________________________

_______________________________

_______________________________

_______________________________

Date:

Request:

_______________________________

_______________________________

_______________________________

Update/Answer:

_______________________________

_______________________________

_______________________________

# Prayer Requests

Date:

Request:

____________________

____________________

____________________

____________________

Update/Answer:

____________________

____________________

____________________

____________________

Date:

Request:

____________________

____________________

____________________

____________________

Update/Answer:

____________________

____________________

____________________

# Prayer Requests

Date:

Request:

_______________________________________

_______________________________________

_______________________________________

_______________________________________

Update/Answer:

_______________________________________

_______________________________________

_______________________________________

_______________________________________

Date:

Request:

_______________________________________

_______________________________________

_______________________________________

Update/Answer:

_______________________________________

_______________________________________

_______________________________________

# Prayer Requests

Date:

Request:

_______________________

_______________________

_______________________

_______________________

Update/Answer:

_______________________

_______________________

_______________________

_______________________

Date:

Request:

_______________________

_______________________

_______________________

_______________________

Update/Answer:

_______________________

_______________________

_______________________

_______________________

# Prayer Requests

Date:

Request:

Update/Answer:

Date:

Request:

Update/Answer:

# Prayer Requests

Date:
Request:

_________________________________________

_________________________________________

_________________________________________

_________________________________________

Update/Answer:

_________________________________________

_________________________________________

_________________________________________

_________________________________________

Date:
Request:

_________________________________________

_________________________________________

_________________________________________

_________________________________________

Update/Answer:

_________________________________________

_________________________________________

_________________________________________

_________________________________________

# Sermon Notes

Date:

Speaker:

# Sermon Notes

Date:
Speaker:

# Sermon Notes

Date:

Speaker:

# Sermon Notes

Date:

Speaker:

# Sermon Notes

Date:

Speaker:

# Notes & Reflections

# Notes & Reflections

Here I am!
I stand at the door and knock.
If anyone hears my voice
and opens the door,
I will come in and
eat with that person,
and they with me.

Revelations 3:20 NIV

# Check-in #12

## Date:

It's time for a monthly reflection and check-in. Remember that each person's prayer journey is unique and personal. Be honest and take time to reflect on your answers.


## MY PRAYER JOURNEY:

Place a mark on the scale below to show where you're at

$\longleftarrow \hspace{8cm} \longrightarrow$

0            5            10

0 = I DON'T REALLY PRAY
5 = I PRAY WHEN I THINK OF IT OR WHEN THERE'S A SPECIFIC NEED
10 = I AM A PRAYER WARRIOR AND PRAY CONTINUOUSLY


## Today I am... (CIRCLE ONE):

SEEING GROWTH IN MY PRAYER LIFE
STRUGGLING WITH:
OTHER:


## What am I grateful for?

What is challenging right now?




How am I showing kindness to myself and others?




Use the space below to write a prayer or draw a picture
as you think about the month ahead.

# Prayer Requests

Date:

Request:

_______________________________________________

_______________________________________________

_______________________________________________

_______________________________________________

Update/Answer:

_______________________________________________

_______________________________________________

_______________________________________________

Date:

Request:

_______________________________________________

_______________________________________________

_______________________________________________

Update/Answer:

_______________________________________________

_______________________________________________

_______________________________________________

# Prayer Requests

Date:

Request:

_______________________________

_______________________________

_______________________________

_______________________________

Update/Answer:

_______________________________

_______________________________

_______________________________

_______________________________

Date:

Request:

_______________________________

_______________________________

_______________________________

_______________________________

Update/Answer:

_______________________________

_______________________________

_______________________________

_______________________________

# Prayer Requests

Date:

Request:

_________________________________

_________________________________

_________________________________

_________________________________

Update/Answer:

_________________________________

_________________________________

_________________________________

_________________________________

Date:

Request:

_________________________________

_________________________________

_________________________________

Update/Answer:

_________________________________

_________________________________

_________________________________

# Prayer Requests

Date:

Request:

_______________________________________

_______________________________________

_______________________________________

_______________________________________

Update/Answer:

_______________________________________

_______________________________________

_______________________________________

_______________________________________

Date:

Request:

_______________________________________

_______________________________________

_______________________________________

_______________________________________

Update/Answer:

_______________________________________

_______________________________________

_______________________________________

_______________________________________

# Prayer Requests

Date:

Request:

_______________________________________________

_______________________________________________

_______________________________________________

_______________________________________________

Update/Answer:

_______________________________________________

_______________________________________________

_______________________________________________

_______________________________________________

Date:

Request:

_______________________________________________

_______________________________________________

_______________________________________________

_______________________________________________

Update/Answer:

_______________________________________________

_______________________________________________

_______________________________________________

_______________________________________________

# Prayer Requests

Date:

Request:

_______________________________

_______________________________

_______________________________

_______________________________

Update/Answer:

_______________________________

_______________________________

_______________________________

_______________________________

Date:

Request:

_______________________________

_______________________________

_______________________________

_______________________________

Update/Answer:

_______________________________

_______________________________

_______________________________

# Prayer Requests

Date:

Request:

_______________________________

_______________________________

_______________________________

_______________________________

Update/Answer:

_______________________________

_______________________________

_______________________________

_______________________________

Date:

Request:

_______________________________

_______________________________

_______________________________

Update/Answer:

_______________________________

_______________________________

_______________________________

# Prayer Requests

Date:

Request:

_______________________________________________

_______________________________________________

_______________________________________________

_______________________________________________

Update/Answer:

_______________________________________________

_______________________________________________

_______________________________________________

_______________________________________________

Date:

Request:

_______________________________________________

_______________________________________________

_______________________________________________

_______________________________________________

Update/Answer:

_______________________________________________

_______________________________________________

_______________________________________________

_______________________________________________

# Sermon Notes

Date:

Speaker:

# Sermon Notes

Date:

Speaker:

# Sermon Notes

Date:

Speaker:

# Sermon Notes

Date:

Speaker:

# Sermon Notes

Date:

Speaker:

# Notes & Reflections

# Notes & Reflections

"

For I know the plans
I have for you,"
declares the Lord,
"plans to prosper you
and not to harm you,
plans to give you hope
and a future.
Then you will call on me
and come
and pray to me,
and I will listen to you.

"

Jeremiah 29:11-12 NIV

# Birthday Reflection

Happy Birthday! May God bless you on your special day!

Take a few moments to thank God for your life and reflect on your prayer journey and relationship with Him.

**How has God revealed Himself to you in the year since your last birthday?**

**How is your prayer journey going?**

**Reflect on how God has blessed you and your loved ones since you celebrated your last birthday.**

**

For the word of the Lord
is right and true;
he is faithful
in all he does.

**

Psalm 33:4 NIV

# Baptism-birthday Reflection

Happy baptism birthday! This check-in is to be done on or around the date your were baptized. If for example you were baptized in July 2011, you would do this check-in July. If you haven't yet been baptized, you can still complete this check-in and reflect on baptism as a public declaration of faith.

Briefly record your baptism story. When and where were you baptized? How old were you? What led you to be baptized?

Reflect on how your relationship with God is different than when you first accepted Jesus Christ as your Lord and savior.

What actionable steps will you take to strengthen your relationship with God over the next year?

But when he,
the Spirit of truth, comes,
he will guide you into all the truth.
He will not speak on his own;
he will speak only what he hears,
and he will tell you
what is yet to come.

John 16:13 NIV

# Closing Reflection

Congratulations! You've made it through a year of prayer, note taking, and reflection. Use this last check-in to reflect and record your thoughts.

What was the biggest blessing of your prayer journey this year?

What was the biggest challenge to your prayer journey?

How has God revealed Himself to you through prayer this year?

Who or what did God use to encourage you?

How has God used you to encourage others?

What area(s) of your life do you want God to transform as you continue to seek Him in prayer?

What commitments will you make or habits will you engage in to seek God, receive His blessings, and love those in your sphere of influence?

Write a prayer of thanksgiving and dedication for continued growth and blessing in the next year.

"

All Scripture is God-breathed
and is useful for teaching,
rebuking, correcting
and training in righteousness,
so that the servant of God
may be thoroughly equipped
for every good work.

"

2 Timothy 3:16-17 NIV

# Scripture References

2 Chronicles 7:14
*"If my people, who are called by my name, will humble themselves and pray and seek my face and turn from their wicked ways, then I will hear from heaven, and I will forgive their sin and will heal their land."*


Psalm 4:1
*"Answer me when I call to you, my righteous God. Give me relief from my distress; have mercy on me and hear my prayer."*


Psalm 33:4
*"For the word of the Lord is right and true; he is faithful in all he does."*


Jeremiah 29:11-12
*"For I know the plans I have for you," declares the Lord, "plans to prosper you and not to harm you, plans to give you hope and a future. Then you will call on me and come and pray to me, and I will listen to you."*


Matthew 5:44-45
*"But I tell you, love your enemies and pray for those who persecute you, that you may be children of your Father in heaven."*


Matthew 7:7-8
*"Ask and it will be given to you; seek and you will find; knock and the door will be opened to you. For everyone who asks receives; the one who seeks finds; and to the one who knocks, the door will be opened."*

*Luke 11:1-4*
*"One day Jesus was praying in a certain place. When he*
*finished, one of his disciples said to him, 'Lord, teach us to pray, just as*
*John taught his disciples.'*

*He said to them, 'When you pray, say:*
*'Father, hallowed be your name, your kingdom come.*
*Give us each day our daily bread.*
*Forgive us our sins, for we also forgive everyone who sins against us.*
*And lead us not into temptation.'"*


*Luke 18:1*
*"Then Jesus told his disciples a parable to show them that they should*
*always pray and not give up."*


*John 16:13*
*"But when he, the Spirit of truth, comes, he will guide you into all the*
*truth. He will not speak on his own; he will speak only what he hears,*
*and he will tell you what is yet to come."*


*Acts 2:42*
*"They devoted themselves to the apostles' teaching and to fellowship,*
*to the breaking of bread and to prayer."*


*Romans 8:26*
*"In the same way, the Spirit helps us in our weakness. We do not know*
*what we ought to pray for, but the Spirit himself intercedes for us*
*through wordless groans."*

*Ephesians 6:18*
*"And pray in the Spirit on all occasions with all kinds of prayers and requests. With this in mind, be alert and always keep on praying for all the Lord's people."*


*Philippians 4:6*
*"Do not be anxious about anything, but in every situation, by prayer and petition, with thanksgiving, present your requests to God."*


*Colossians 4:2*
*"Devote yourselves to prayer, being watchful and thankful."*


*2 Timothy 3:16-17*
*"All Scripture is God-breathed and is useful for teaching, rebuking, correcting and training in righteousness, so that the servant of God may be thoroughly equipped for every good work."*


*James 5:16*
*"Therefore confess your sins to each other and pray for each other so that you may be healed. The prayer of a righteous person is powerful and effective."*


*Revelations 3:20*
*"Here I am! I stand at the door and knock. If anyone hears my voice and opens the door, I will come in and eat with that person, and they with me."*

Psalm 63:1-8
"You, God, are my God,
    earnestly I seek you;
I thirst for you,
    my whole being longs for you,
in a dry and parched land
    where there is no water.

I have seen you in the sanctuary
    and beheld your power and your glory.
Because your love is better than life,
    my lips will glorify you.
 I will praise you as long as I live,
    and in your name I will lift up my hands.
 I will be fully satisfied as with the richest of foods;
    with singing lips my mouth will praise you.

On my bed I remember you;
    I think of you through the watches of the night.
Because you are my help,
    I sing in the shadow of your wings.
I cling to you;
    your right hand upholds me."


Numbers 6:24-26
""'The Lord bless you and keep you;
the Lord make his face shine on you and be gracious to you;
the Lord turn his face toward you and give you peace."'

# Notes & Reflections

# Notes & Reflections

# Notes & Reflections

# Notes & Reflections

# Notes & Reflections

# Notes & Reflections

# Notes & Reflections

# Notes & Reflections

# Notes & Reflections

# Notes & Reflections

# Notes & Reflections

# Notes & Reflections

# Notes & Reflections

# Notes & Reflections

# Notes & Reflections

# Notes & Reflections

# Notes & Reflections

# Notes & Reflections

# Notes & Reflections

# Notes & Reflections

# Notes & Reflections

# Notes & Reflections